A Cup o,
Mint
Tea

Knowledge, Trust, and Other
Short Stories to Warm the Heart

Volume 5

BY IMAN ABDALLAH AL-QAISI

Illustrator
Nadia Yousef

Translator
Maha Ezzeddine

Copy Editor
Sumaiya Susan Gavell
(Sterling International Editors)

Layout and Graphics
Zaid Al-Dabbagh
(Panda UX Studio Limited)

PANDAUX
WEB APPS + UI/UX DESIGN + USABILITY/ACCESSIBILITY
WWW.PANDAUX.CO

Acknowledgments

Our sincere gratitude to God, first and foremost, for blessing this project, bringing it to fruition, and expanding it far beyond our expectations. All praise to God, Lord of the Worlds.

We would also like to thank all of those who supported this project in various ways. Because of your hard work, sincere advice, thoughtful prayers, and encouraging words, this project has been able to continue for five years. By purchasing the collections, reading through the volumes, and sharing it with others, you have made this project greatly successful, all praise to God.

Special thanks to Freda Shamma, Hadia Mahmoud, Hanan Abu Salah, and Shorouq Alhayek for your assistance in our moments of need.

Introduction

"A joy to the reader, another volume of Iman Al-Qaisi's *A Cup of Mint Tea* has arrived. As only one long devoted to Islamic learning might do, the author has revived and regenerated lessons from the Quran and the Islamic tradition, encapsulating them in accessible stories, engaging and easy to understand. Another volume adds to this glowing collection, an invitation to all!"

— *Sumaiya Susan Gavell*

CONTENTS

God says

"Worship God, and do not associate anything with Him, and be good to parents and to kin and orphans and the needy and the close neighbor(s) and the distant neighbor(s) and the companion at your side and the traveler and to those owned by you. Surely, God does not like those who are arrogant and proud."

[Al-Nisa':36]

— 1 —
The Rude Neighbor
Forbearance and Patience [1]

There once was a righteous man named Sahl Ibn Abdullah At-Tustari, may God be pleased with him. He lived in an apartment below his neighbor, who was a fire-worshipper who disbelieved in God. In the ceiling of Sahl's home was an opening between the two apartments, of which the upstairs neighbor was unaware. The man was in the habit of dumping his household and personal waste into this opening. The waste landed right in the middle of Sahl's home.

Instead of confronting his neighbor, Sahl placed a bucket underneath the opening. Every night, Sahl would carry the bucket some distance from the house to dispose of his neighbor's waste. This continued for many years.

Finally, Sahl became ill and knew that his death was imminent.

---

[1] Al-Kaba'ir by Imam Al-Dhahabi, as well as Anees As-Saliheen wa Sameer Al-Muttaqeen.

He summoned his neighbor and told him, "Look into my house and find the opening in the ceiling."

The neighbor did so, then asked, "What about it?"

"For many years, the waste from your home has fallen through that opening into my house. I have collected it in a bucket during the day and disposed of it every night. I would not have complained to you, except that my time has come, and I fear that another neighbor will not tolerate your practice. Do whatever you see fit," Sahl said kindly.

The neighbor was silent for a few moments and then said, "Honorable *Shaikh*, you have treated me with such patience, even though I caused much trouble for you and was a disbeliever in God. Please, give me your hand."

"I bear witness that there is no one worthy of worship except God, and that Muhammad is the Messenger of God," said the neighbor. After witnessing the testimony of faith from his neighbor, Sahl passed away.

Lessons Learned:

1. **Showing Patience When Harmed Is a Form of Worship**

   Sahl obeyed God by displaying patience with the unintentional harm inflicted upon him by his neighbor. He was patient for a prolonged time in the hope of gaining God's favor. God says, "Obey God and His Messenger, and do not quarrel with each other, lest you should lose courage, and your prowess should evaporate; and be patient. Surely, God is with the patient."[2] Do not assume that fasting, prayer, and remembrance are the only forms of worship. Good treatment toward others, kindness to neighbors, and acts of patience can be the greatest forms of worship.

2. **Kindness to Neighbors Shows Strong Faith**

   This righteous man applied the teaching of Prophet Muhammad (s): "Whoever believes in God and the Last Day should be good to his neighbor."[3] Sahl was very good to his neighbor. Use the art of neighborliness to practice refinement and kindness to those nearby. Never forget that kind treatment is one of the best ways to draw closer to God and find His mercy, blessings, and compassion.

3. **Demand the Best from Oneself, but Do Not Be Demanding of Others**

   From his keen wisdom and sharp understanding, Sahl showed great self-control while enduring the harm inflicted upon him by his neighbor. It would have been reasonable for him to have raised the issue with his neighbor from the very first incident. Instead, he patiently suffered the harm. He confronted his

---

[2] [Al-Anfal:46]

[3] Muslim.

4

neighbor only as he neared death, when he could not expect his children and family members to continue to carry the burden as he had done. Remember that if you expect loyalty from your children, ask of them what is reasonable. Do not burden others with more than they will be able to handle, for you might lose them in the end, and God knows best.

4. Good Character Earns a Variety of Blessings

Firstly, Sahl's good character led to the guidance of the fire-worshipper. The Prophet (s) swore, "By God, were God to guide a single man through you, it would be better for you than a herd of red camels."[4] Secondly, every deed of the newly guided man would also be awarded to the righteous man who had guided him. Thirdly, Sahl set a good example for others to follow, so once again he would be generously rewarded. Treat people well and receive a reward that is beyond count or measure, God willing.

---

[4] Bukhari, Muslim.

The Prophet (s) said

_____

"By God, he does not believe! By God, he does not believe!" It was asked, "Who is that, Oh Messenger of God?" He said, "That person whose neighbor does not feel safe from his evil."

_____

Related by Abu Hurairah
(Agreed Upon)

— 2 —
Abu Hanifa and His Neighbor
Kindness to Neighbors[5]

Abu Hanifa An-Nu'man, one of the greatest scholars in the history of Islam, lived in the city of Kufa. He happened to live next door to a very troublesome neighbor. This neighbor spent his nights in a drunken stupor, singing at the top his lungs. He composed long songs and poetry, lamenting his loneliness.

"They've abandoned me, and what a person have they abandoned! I would have stood bravely in battle and siege ..." wailed the neighbor.

The drunkard sang night after night, so much that Abu Hanifa memorized his songs by heart. The drunkard's singing grew so irksome that a city official heard and arrested the neighbor for drinking and public disturbance.

[5] Ahsan al-Qisas, vol. 4 pg. 29-30,by Ali Fikri.

The next night, Abu Hanifa was surprised to hear nothing but silence from his neighbor's home. Worried, Abu Hanifa knocked on the door but found no one inside. Any other person might have enjoyed the peace and quiet, but not Abu Hanifa.

"Where is my neighbor? I have missed his voice," inquired Abu Hanifa of the people on his street. It was not long before Abu Hanifa discovered what had happened.

Abu Hanifa invited his neighbors and companions to accompany him, saying, "We must go and save our neighbor from prison! It is our obligation. The Prophet (s) urged us to take care of our neighbors."

When Abu Hanifa entered the city hall of Kufa, a hush fell upon the gathering. The respected Imam Abu Hanifa himself! The governor stepped down from his chair, greeted Abu Hanifa, took him by the hand, and welcomed him personally.

"To what do we owe this honor, Imam Abu Hanifa? You could have sent us a message, for your time is better spent in learning, writing, and teaching."

The Imam replied, "My neighbor is a prisoner. The guards took him yesterday, and I have come to ask that you release him. I would like you to entrust him to me."

The surprised governor agreed. "I will free him, of course. And in honor of your visit, all of the prisoners held in our jail tonight will be freed."

As soon as the neighbor was released and was alone with Abu Hanifa, the scholar questioned him using a verse from his nightly songs: "Have we abandoned you, my friend?"

Abashed, the neighbor replied, "No, Sir, your honor! You have certainly not abandoned me. I will never do anything to harm you again."

Abu Hanifa placed a bag of ten dinars in his neighbor's hand. He told him to use the money to pay for any loss of income that he might have incurred due to his night in prison. "And whenever you are in need of anything, come to me. Do not let there be any shyness between us," said the Imam.

The neighbor kissed the forehead of Abu Hanifa. After that night, he started to attend the Imam's lessons as a dedicated student. Soon, Abu Hanifa's neighbor became one of Kufa's finest scholars.

Lessons Learned:

1. Intoxicants Are a Source of Corruption

The neighbor was known for his immoral behavior. The habit of drinking caused his loss of intellect, disruptive behavior, violation of the rights of others, clamor, obnoxious singing, and bad language. Because his mind was absent, there was no limit to the physical and verbal harm he would cause. These are just a few logical reasons that God has forbidden alcohol. God says, "Oh you who believe! Wine, gambling, altars and divining arrows are filth, made up by Satan. Therefore, refrain from [them], so that you may be successful."[6] Keep a distance from the traps of intoxicants, and those who are addicted to them. They can drag someone with them into the fire, God forbid.

2. Repetition Aids Memorization

Abu Hanifa memorized the poetry of his neighbor, despite finding it distasteful and disruptive. Parents should remember that the repetition of words of wisdom to their children is important, even if it appears that the children do not hear or heed their parents' advice. The day will come for all parents when they will discover good habits in their children that prove that they were in fact listening all along. Similarly, hearing bad language from friends or relatives will undoubtedly have an effect. No one is immune, as the old saying confirms: "Whoever spends forty days with a people has become one of them." Be honorable with others, take in only what is beneficial, and keep a distance from bad company who might cause one to perish.

---

[6] [Al-Ma'idah:90]

3. The Honored Rights of the Neighbor in Islam

Abu Hanifa checked on his neighbor because he knew that God advised him to do so. As the Prophet (s) said, "Gabriel continued to advise me to treat neighbors well until I thought he would make them my heirs."[7] The scholars mentioned the rights of the neighbor: "Feed him from what you eat, help him when he asks for help, visit him when he is sick, get happy for his happiness and sad for his sadness, and do not build a high fence that could block his view." May God make all those who fear Him understand their neighborly duties, through which they can draw closer to Him.

4. Nations Rise When Scholars Are Respected

The governor honored and respected Imam Abu Hanifa, which was clear when he fulfilled Abu Hanifa's request to release his neighbor. This was done out of honor and respect for the Imam's lofty status. The leader was aware that God honors the scholars and has placed them on par with the angels. As God said, "God bears witness that there is no god but He, and (so do) the angels and the men of knowledge, being the One who maintains equity. There is no god but He, the Mighty, the Wise."[8] Always remember that only great and prosperous nations respect their scholars, and that honoring scholars brings success and happiness in this life and the next, God willing.

5. Good Treatment Rectifies the Mind and Heart

Abu Hanifa offered good treatment and kind words to his neighbor when he expressed, "We will not abandon you." Abu Hanifa even gave his neighbor money, and he reminded him that he would be there for him if he needed anything. This exceptional treatment

---

[7] Agreed Upon.
[8] [Al-Imran:18]

deeply touched the neighbor and brought him to detest his own poor behavior. The neighbor changed his understanding and became a strong believer who studied and taught sacred knowledge. As God has mentioned, "Is there any reward for goodness other than goodness?"[9] Be among the people of goodness, and strive to win in this world and the next, God willing.

[9] [Ar-Rahman:60]

The Prophet (s) said

"If you guarantee me six things on your behalf,
I shall guarantee you Paradise: speak the truth
when you talk, keep a promise when you make
one, fulfill the trust when you are entrusted
with something, protect your chastity, lower
your gaze, and restrain your hands from
harming others."

Related by Ubada Ibn Samit
(Narrated by Ahmed)

— 3 —
The Honest Shepherd
Trustworthiness [10]

Nafi', a scholar and servant of Abdullah Ibn Umar (ra)[*], one of the well known companions, tells this story:

Several friends and I went with Abdullah Ibn Umar to the countryside surrounding Medina. We prepared a delicious meal out in the open desert. As we prepared to eat, a shepherd and his flock passed us by.

Abdullah Ibn Umar beckoned the shepherd and said, "Come, shepherd, and eat with us!"

"I am fasting!" replied the shepherd, and he continued

---

[10] Sifat As-Safwa, vol. 2 p. 188, by Ibn Al-Jawzi.

[*] Acronym for "*radiyya Allahu anhu,*" or "may God be pleased with him." Common Islamic etiquette encourages such prayers to be made for the companions of the Prophet (s) at the written or spoken mention of their names.

on his way.

"On a day like this?" Abdullah Ibn Umar called out after him. "You guide your sheep up and down the mountainside under the hot sun. Why would you fast in such weather?"

The shepherd shrugged. "Fasting keeps me occupied on these long, empty days," he replied. Abdullah Ibn Umar was intrigued. He made the shepherd a proposition.

"What if we were to buy one of your sheep from you? We will slaughter it and cook it over our fire. You can eat its meat and share in our meal, and you will also be able to keep the price of your sheep!" said Ibn Umar.

The shepherd shook his head. "These animals do not belong to me. They belong to my master."

"Would it be so wrong?" challenged Ibn Umar. "You can tell your master that a wolf killed the sheep. He would never know the truth."

The shepherd turned away, raising his finger to the sky. "Where, then, is God?" He rounded up his flock and disappeared into the hills.

For the rest of the day, Abdullah Ibn Umar murmured incredulously to himself, "Indeed. The shepherd asked, 'Where is God?'"

When the party returned to Medina, Ibn Umar sent a letter to the shepherd's master. He included enough money to purchase the shepherd and his flock. Without hesitation, Ibn Umar set the trustworthy shepherd free and gifted him the flock of sheep.

Lessons Learned:

1. An Hour in the "Shade" of Obedience

The Prophet (s)[11], his companions, and his followers understood the importance of educating people beyond the walls of the mosque. They ventured out, gathering with others to enjoy food and good company. By doing so, they found a balance in nourishing the body and the soul. The Prophet (s) advised us, "Your Lord has a right over you, your body has a right over you, and your family has a right over you, so give each one his due."[12] Spend time in good company, break bread together, and always remember to dedicate a portion of the gathering to gratitude, reflection, or the remembrance of God.

2. Feeding People Is an Act of the Righteous

Ibn Umar wanted to honor the shepherd and gain reward when he invited him to come eat with the group. God describes the righteous as such: "And they give food, out of their love for Him (God), to the needy, and the orphan, and the captive."[13] Therefore, make it a habit to invite others to whatever you may have to eat. Do not squander the reward or the opportunity to increase the love between you.

3. Voluntary Fasting Is an Act of the God-Fearing

Ibn Umar noticed signs of deep faith in the shepherd. When he asked the shepherd about fasting on a very hot day, he implied that he made good use of his time by doing acts of devotion to prepare for the Day of

---

[11] Abbreviation for "*salla Allahu alayhi wa sallam,*" or "peace be upon him." Common Islamic etiquette dictates prayers of peace to be made for the Prophet Muhammad (s) at every written or spoken mention of his beloved name.

[12] Bukhari, no.1867.

[13] [Al-Insaan:8]

Judgment. Be of those who make good use of their time, consistently do good deeds, and make up for mistakes often long forgotten, and be of those who fast often.

4. Faith Is Expressed in Actions before Words

Abdullah wanted to give the shepherd a challenging test. He tested him with wealth by proposing to buy a sheep, pocket the money, and claim that the wolf had eaten the missing livestock. Yet the shepherd proved a powerful point, that faith is not merely words, but rather words and actions. The shepherd was following the words of God, "Does he not know that God is watching (him)?"[14]

5. Trustworthiness Is a Quality of the God-Fearing

The shepherd understood his responsibility as the trustee of the flock. He would not allow a single sheep to go missing. Today, it is rare to find those who have such ethics and embody this lofty sense of responsibility. Too often, people waste valuable work time playing on their phones, sending messages, or socializing with friends during paid company time. Time allotted for work, as promised and agreed to in contract, feeds and sustains one's family. Do not forget that such oversight also wrongs God, as He says, "Oh you who believe, do not betray the trust of God and the Messenger, and do not betray your mutual trusts, while you know."[15]

6. When Letting Go for the Sake of God, God Compensates with Better

The shepherd refused to accept payment for a single sheep, so God granted him not only the entire flock, but he gained his freedom as well. Fear God and be trustworthy, and God will always compensate beyond expectation, God willing.

---

[14] [Al-Alaq:14]
[15] [Al-Anfal:27]

17

The Prophet (s) said

"A man bought a piece of land from another man, and the buyer found a jar filled with gold in the land. The buyer said to the seller: 'Take your gold, as I bought only the land from you and not the gold.' The owner of the land said: 'I sold you the land with everything in it.' So both of them took their case before a third man who asked: 'Have you any children?' One of them said: 'I have a boy.' The other said: 'I have a girl.' The man said: 'Marry the girl to the boy and spend the money on them; and whatever remains give it in charity.'"

Related by Abu Hurairah
(Narrated by Bukhari and Muslim)

— 4 —
The Jar of Gold
Honesty and Trustworthiness [16]

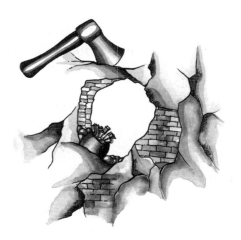

Once there lived an honest merchant. He remained conscious of God at all times and feared disobeying Him. After many years of hard work, the merchant grew old and weary. He decided it was time to retire from the merchant's trade.

Back in his hometown, the retired merchant bought a suitable house. After some time in his comfortable dwelling, the merchant became restless. Taking a critical look at the home, he thought, "If I knock down some of these walls, the house would be more spacious!"

It was not long before the merchant, with axe in hand, demolished one of the walls of his home. As the wall

---

[16] Story is based on an authentic *hadith** of Prophet Muhammad (s).
* A *hadith* is a carefully recorded saying of the Prophet Muhammad (s).

crumbled away, he noticed something hidden in the rubble, tucked between the bricks. The merchant carefully dislodged a clay jar from the wall, and to his astonishment, he found it to be full of gold!

"A jar of gold!" exclaimed the merchant. "I must return this to the former owner of the house!" The man did not consider for even a moment to keep the treasure for himself. He knew that any wealth obtained unjustly could only be a curse and a source of misery.

So the honest merchant carried the jar full of gold to the former owner of the house and presented it to him.

"This jar of gold belongs to you," the merchant said. "I found it hidden inside a wall of the house you sold to me."

The previous owner, also an honest and God-fearing man, smiled and shook his head. "No, I sold you the house, which included everything inside. So the jar of gold belongs to you."

The merchant was surprised. He could not accept such great wealth. He argued with the former owner, and the former owner argued back. Neither man would accept the treasure, for neither man would risk violating the rights of the other. Unable to reach a resolution, the two men decided to consult the local judge.

After hearing the story of the jar, the judge shook his head in utter disbelief. He had never seen more trustworthy men than the two before him.

The judge asked, "Do you have any unmarried children?"

The merchant answered that he had a daughter, while

the house's former owner had a son.

"Marry your children to each other," said the judge. "And spend the treasure on their marriage."

The two men agreed that the judge's ruling was most fair and appropriate. So it was that the two trustworthy, God-fearing families soon became one.

Lessons Learned:

1. **The Necessity and Importance of Preparing for the Future**

   Previously, early Muslims thoughtfully prepared for the later days of their lives, similar to the manner used in developed societies today. This merchant planned his personal finances for his upcoming elderly years. He prepared financially by setting aside some funds in a nest egg, and he prepared physically by settling in a suitable home so that he would not have the physical burden of moving later. Islam also teaches us to prepare spiritually, as aging draws one closer to meeting God. The elderly should be especially focused on doing good deeds, because this type of "insurance" guarantees success in this life and the next.

2. **Renovation Spreads Comfort and Joy to the Soul**

   The merchant tried to improve his life by expanding and renovating his home. Modern psychologists have found that minor changes to a person's environment can have dramatic psychological effects. This shows in the happiness and well-being of family life. Do not get stuck in mindless routines, but rather change habits and rituals from time to time. This will bring dramatic improvement to oneself and others.

3. **Strong Work Habits Benefit Health and Well-Being**

   Despite his old age and his financial ability to hire a worker, the merchant chose to demolish the wall himself. He understood that God prefers hands that work hard. This is confirmed by what the Prophet (s) said when he shook a man's hand and found it to be rough from hard manual labor. The Prophet (s) said, "This hand is loved by God and his Prophet (s)." Be of those who work actively to win the love of God and his Prophet (s), and to maintain health and strength.

4. Trustworthiness Always Brings out the Good

The merchant could have easily justified pocketing the found treasure. He had purchased the home, and understandably, with the house came everything that was in it. Yet he hoped to return the forgotten funds to the previous owner out of fear that he had violated the rights of another. He put into practice the verse, "Oh you who believe, do not betray the trust of God and the Messenger, and do not betray your mutual trusts, while you know. Be aware that your wealth and your children are but a trial and that with God there is a great reward."[17] Because of the honesty and trustworthiness of the merchant, he was given not only the gold, but he was also blessed with a righteous husband for his daughter. Be trustworthy, and welcome God's abundant blessings in wealth and children to follow. The greatest reward is still awaiting in the the Hereafter.

---

[17] [Al-Anfal:27-28]

God says

"Did you not see a group from the Children of Israel, after (the time of) Moses when they said to their prophet: 'Appoint for us a king, so that we may fight in the way of God.' He said: 'Is it (not) likely, if fighting is enjoined upon you, that you would not fight?' They said: 'What is wrong with us, that we would not fight while we have been driven away from our homes and our sons?' But, when fighting was enjoined upon them, they turned away, except a few of them, and God is aware of the unjust. Their prophet said to them: 'God has appointed Saul (Talut) as a king for you.' They said: 'How could he have kingship over us when we are more entitled to the kingship than him? He has not been given affluence in wealth.' He said: 'God has chosen him over you and has increased his stature in knowledge and physique, and God gives His kingship to whom He wills. God is All-Embracing, All-Knowing." Their prophet said to them: 'The sign of his kingship is that the Ark shall come to you, carried by the angels, having in it tranquility from your Lord, and the remains of what the house of Moses and the house of Aaron (Harun) had left. Surely, in it there is a sign for you, if you are believers.' So, when Saul (Talut) set out along with the troops, he said: 'God is going to test you by a river, so, whoever drinks from it is not my man, and whoever does not taste it is surely a man of mine, except the one who scoops a little with his hand.' Then they drank from it, except a few of them. So, when it (the river) was crossed by him and by those who believed with him, they said: 'There is no strength with us today against Goliath (Jalut) and his troops.' Said those who believed in having to meet God: 'How many small groups have overcome large groups by the will of God. God is with those who remain patient.' And when they faced Goliath (Jalut) and his troops, they said: 'Our Lord, pour endurance upon us, make firm our feet, and help us against the disbelieving people.' So, they defeated them by the will of God, and David (Dawud) killed Goliath (Jalut), and God gave him the kingdom and the wisdom and taught him what He willed. Had God not been pushing back some people by means of others, the earth would have been spoiled. But God is All-Gracious to all the worlds."

[Al-Baqarah:246-251]

— 5 —
Saul (Talut) the King
Belief in Prophets [19]

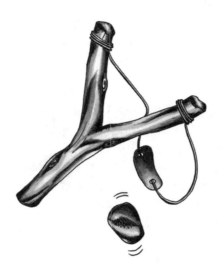

The Children of Israel (*Bani Israil*), the tribe of Moses (as)*, conquered Palestine under the leadership of Joshua (*Yusha Ibn Nun* (as)). They settled there, worshipping God as Moses had taught them. But after a time, the Children of Israel returned to a life of disobedience and corruption. They went astray from the path of Moses and denied the blessings of God. So God made them fall under the rule of a ruthless, powerful king named Goliath, or *Jalut* in Arabic. Goliath killed the men from the Children of Israel and took the women and children as captives. He expelled them from

---

[19] Ma Al-Anbiyaa fi al-Quran al-Kareem, pg. 272-278, by Afeef Abdullah Al-Fattah Tabbarah.

* Acronym for "*alayhi as-salat wa as-salam*," or "upon him be prayers and peace." Common Islamic etiquette encourages prayers of peace to be made for the prophets at the written or spoken mention of their names.

their homes and rendered them defenseless. Their sacred treasures, the tablets and the Covenant Ark, a wooden chest containing the relics of Moses, were confiscated from the Children of Israel.

Even in their weakened state, the Children of Israel longed to fight Goliath and be free from his oppression. They had no leadership or strategy, but they were given a prophet. So they begged their prophet to appoint a king for the Children of Israel who would lead them in victory against their oppressors.

Their prophet was worried about this request. If God had appointed a king, then supporting and fighting alongside this king would be an obligation. Would his soldiers be able to meet the challenge, or would they cower in battle? But the Children of Israel were adamant. They wanted a king who would lead them in battle, and they would stand by him no matter how great the challenge.

So God revealed to their prophet that Saul (*Talut*) was to be the king of the Children of Israel.

The people cried out in dismay. They neither expected nor desired such a king as Saul. Saul was a simple man and a member of one of the lower classes. The rich and elite of the Children of Israel had secretly hoped that one of them would be chosen for the title. More important to them than victory was the power and influence of being king.

Their prophet was adamant: Saul was God's choice for king. He was strong in body and wise in mind. To further convince the Children of Israel, Saul was to come with a sign. The angels themselves would bring Saul the Covenant Ark, a wooden chest containing the treasures of Moses, which Goliath had stolen. As the people looked on, the angels presented the precious relics of the Children of Israel to their new king. There could be no doubt that Saul had been appointed by God, and the Children of Israel had no choice but to accept him as their ruler. God then commanded the people to follow Saul in his march against the tyrant who had humiliated and oppressed them.

It soon became clear that many of the people had no intention of actually fighting. A few men, however, readied for battle and marched with Saul. They were prepared to face Goliath and his massive forces, despite their small numbers. With this small band of believing soldiers, Saul set across a desert route upon which there was no water. The army soldiers protested; the thirst and exhaustion was impossible to survive. Saul, their king, reassured them that if they continued their march with patience and steadfastness, they would find a river just ahead.

However, Saul gave the group firm instructions: when they reached the river, they were not to drink from it. Only a small, quick sip from the hand was allowed. Soon, the small army found themselves at the banks of the river. Many could not control themselves and drank from the water without restraint.

Saul ordered everyone who had drunk more than a sip from the river to leave the army and head back home. The number of soldiers dwindled even further. The small army crossed the river to where the enemy forces awaited. At this moment, some of the soldiers who had to this point been patient and steadfast hesitated. How could such a small group possibly overcome the strength and power of Goliath and his army?

The doubt became so great in the soldiers' hearts that yet

again, some turned on their heels in fear at the last moment. Those who remained were the ones whose faith was strong and unshakeable. They raised their hands in supplication, saying, "God, pour patience upon us, make our footsteps firm, and grant us victory over those who disbelieve."[20]

The two armies stood facing each other. Goliath, armed to the teeth and formidable in his layers of metal armor, paraded proudly, mounted upon his horse.

"Who will challenge me to a duel? Who will fight me?" he bellowed.

Within Saul's army was a young man, a brave soldier from the descendants of Abraham, whose name was David. It was his voice which was raised in response to Goliath, and it was he who stepped into the arena for the duel. He aimed his slingshot at the powerful king and his aim rang true. The mighty Goliath was killed by a boy and his stone.

Witnessing their king defeated so quickly, Goliath's forces fled the battlefield. The brave army of believers was victorious, with the help of God, despite their small numbers. A new era, free from oppression and humiliation, began for the Children of Israel. God says in the Quran, "And so with God's permission they defeated them. David killed Goliath, and God gave him sovereignty and wisdom and taught him what He pleased."[21]

---

[20] [Al-Baqarah:250]
[21] [Al-Baqarah:251]

Lessons Learned:

1. God Places Greater Oppressors over the Corrupt on Earth

The story teaches a powerful lesson, and those who understand it will never oppress others. God places an oppressor such as Goliath and his army over those who stray far from the path of truth and who spread corruption. Spread righteousness so that God may love you and put such love in the hearts of his servants. Do not sow corruption or encourage oppression by remaining silent about the oppression of other people.

2. Breaking Promises Is the Character of Hypocrites

This story teaches that one's words are promises. Keeping such promises is a trait of the believer. Many people become excited when they hear a new idea and are quick to make promises, but when the time comes to do the real work, few follow through. God clarifies this: "Did you not see a group from the Children of Israel, after (the time of) Moses when they said to their prophet: 'Appoint for us a king, so that we may fight in the way of God.' He said: 'Is it (not) likely, if fighting is enjoined upon you, that you would not fight?' They said: 'What is wrong with us that we would not fight while we have been driven away from our homes and our sons?' But, when fighting was enjoined upon them, they turned away, except a few of them, and God is Aware of the unjust."[22] Be of those who speak with intention and follow through on their words. Remember that words are promises, so always fulfill verbal commitments, and God knows best.

---

[22] [Al-Baqarah:246]

3. Strength and Wisdom Are Qualities of Leadership

Throughout history, powerful countries and successful businesses have naturally been led by the wealthy, connected, and elite. Yet God challenges this notion and common assumption. Instead, He presents two important qualities for leadership: The first is a combination of knowledge and wisdom, critical for making big decisions and following through. The second is to possess inner and outer strength. In the past, a leader's physical strength of body could intimidate the enemy and draw fear and respect from other leaders. Today, inner strength is vital. Maintaining a demeanor that reflects a strong commitment to important causes is particularly important in leadership. Good leaders, past and present, always possess a timeless strength of integrity. Do not forget the importance of these two qualities when choosing leaders.

4. Listening and Obeying Unifies the Ranks of the Believers

Saul required something unexplainable from his army, restricting them to a handful of water at the river. He did so to confirm their sincerity, resilience, and faith. Many did not obey the orders due to their lack of understanding or fleeting patience. No matter what the circumstance is, recognize that under the leadership of superiors, subordinates should follow their lead and take their orders. Debating, objecting, and undermining often develop into destructive conflicts amidst the ranks of the believers, and this can cause irreparable damage. This in no way suggests that citizens should blindly obey or even tolerate oppressive, tyrannical leaders. Rather, it reminds citizens and employees to select leaders who can be trusted in their decision-making, leaders who may later be held accountable for their decisions. There is no need, then, to debate every decision or demand extensive explanations at every step if qualified leaders were chosen in the first place. As long as there is mutual faith, trust, and care, building for the greater good of the community will be the common focus, and God knows best.

5. Sincere Intentions and Patience Bring Victory

When Saul made his army practice patience in thirst and in meeting the enemy, they prayed to God to renew their intentions. Then God granted them victory. God says, "And when they faced *Jalut* (Goliath) and his troops, they said: 'Our Lord, pour out endurance on us, make firm our feet and help us against the disbelieving people.'"[23] Use these three powerful tools: Firstly, purify one's intentions, ensuring that one's work and decisions are truly for the sake of God. Secondly, ask for the task to be easy, accept the circumstances, and appreciate the struggle. Thirdly, be patient and realize that victory rarely comes on the first try.

6. The Behavior of Believers under Extreme Conditions

The believers in this army displayed their firmness and loyalty to one another. They became an example for people of all eras, as they obtained victory not by their numbers, but rather by their faith and commitment. God supports the patient minority: "Said those who believed in their having to meet God: 'How many small groups have overcome large groups by the will of God? God is with those who remain patient.'"[24] Do not focus on a majority led by falsehood, who persistently remain silent in the face of truth.

---

[23] [Al-Baqarah:250]
[24] [Al-Baqarah:249]

God says

"All men used to be a single Ummah (on a single faith). Then (after they differed in matters of faith), God sent prophets carrying good news and warning, and sent down with them the Book with truth to judge between people in matters of their dispute. But it was no other than those to whom it (the Book) was given who, led by envy against each other, disputed it after the clear signs had come to them. Then God, by His will, guided those who believed to the truth over which they disputed; and God guides whom He wills to the straight path."

[Al-Baqarah:213]

— 6 —

Ninety-Nine Sheep

Belief in the Books [25]

After the victory for the Children of Israel (*Bani Israil*) over Goliath, David (as) was appointed king of his people. God granted David both the honor of kingship and prophethood. God revealed to David (as) the Psalms, or *Zabur*, a holy book containing wisdoms and reminders from God, as mentioned in the Quran, "And we gave David the Psalms."[26]

God also blessed David with a most beautiful voice, unparalleled by any other human. When David read the Psalms and recited the praises of God, birds would descend and join him in praise. The mountains would join David's recitation every morning and evening. In the Quran, God describes "We made the mountains join him in glorifying Us

---

[25] Ma Al-Anbiyaa fi al-Quran al-Kareem, pg. 279-382, by Afeef Abdullah Al-Fattah Tabbarah.
[26] [Al-Nisa:163]

at sunset and sunrise; and the birds, too, in flocks, all turned to God with him."[27] God gave David other blessings too. He was taught how to shape and weld iron, a skill which had been unknown until that time. David and his people mastered the art of making armor and weapons.

The Quran tells us an intriguing story about Prophet David. One day he was sitting in his place of prayer, worshipping and praying, when two men climbed the wall of his retreat and approached him. David was startled by this unexpected entrance, but the two men reassured him.

"We are just two men who have a dispute. We have come so that you might judge rightly between us," they said.

David asked the men to tell their story.

The first man said, "This is my brother. He has ninety-nine sheep, while I have only one. But he demands that I give him my only sheep so he may have all of the one-hundred."

David immediately concluded that the first man was treated unjustly, and that the fault lay with the owner of the ninety-nine sheep.

David said, "He has wronged you by demanding that you add your sheep to his flock!"

As soon as David pronounced his judgment, the two men vanished suddenly into thin air. David realized that the two men were angels, and that this had been a test from God. David recognized his mistake; he had not listened to what the second man had to say before coming to a judgment. Without hesitation, David sought God's forgiveness and repented for his mistake.

---

[27] [Sad:18-19]

Prophet David was recognized by God for his constant praise, supplication, and prayers. God describes David's continuous devotion in the Quran: "Remember our servant David, a man of strength who always turned to Us."[28] Prophet Muhammad (s) said about David, "He was the person who worshipped God the most."[29] He (s) also said in a hadith, "The most beloved type of fasting to God is the 'Fast of David,' which is to fast every other day. The most beloved prayer to God is the 'Prayer of David.' He would sleep the first half of the night, pray for one-third, then sleep for the last sixth."[30]

David was self-sufficient, living on what his own hands had earned. When he eventually died, his son Solomon became a king and a prophet after him. God says in the Quran, "Solomon succeeded David. He said, 'People, we have been taught the speech of birds, and we have been given a share of everything: this is clearly a great favor.'"[31]

[28] [Sad:17]
[29] Bukhari.
[30] Agreed Upon.
[31] [Al-Naml:16]

Lessons Learned:

1. ## Victory Generates Power and Greatness

   The victory of David (as) in battle taught him to have leadership, which gave him strength and greatness. After the death of Saul, the Children of Israel appointed David as king, and God granted him prophethood. God mentions, "By God's will, they routed them: and David slew Goliath; and God gave him power and wisdom and taught him whatever else He willed. And did not God check one set of people by means of another, the earth would indeed be full of mischief, but God is full of bounty to all the worlds."[32]

2. ## Divine Books Are Miracles of the Prophets

   God has honored the prophets by giving them unique miracles. Perhaps among the greatest and most lasting miracles are the books that have continued to influence and shape believers long after the prophets' deaths. The divine books sent down from God to His prophets include the Scrolls (*Suhuf*), the Torah (*Tawrat*), the Psalms (*Zabur*), the Bible (*Injil*), and the Quran. The Psalms contained rules and regulations sent down by God to structure their lives with purpose and to rectify nations for the world to prosper. The corruption or destruction of a nation is usually the result of people disregarding necessary laws, rules, and regulations. Be among those who bring positive solutions through reform, and not among those who bring destruction.

3. ## Gratitude Is Characteristic of the Prophets

   When David (as) was granted victory, became king, then became a prophet, he displayed his gratitude to

---

[32] [Al-Baqarah:251]

God through acts of worship. He often recited the Psalms, remembering and glorifying God morning and evening. He would stay up one-third of the night in prayer, and he would fast every other day. He drew close to God with such deeds, so God blessed him with many miracles. David could shape iron, and the birds and the mountains glorified God with him. Every form of good that blesses a person stems from growing close to God, as God has said, "If you express gratitude, I shall certainly give you more, and if you are ungrateful, then My punishment is indeed severe."[33]

4. Trials Are Lessons as well as Purification

God wanted to test David and teach him that spiritual and physical worship is not enough to bring success or contentment. Trials and tribulations are necessary to return every servant back to God, and to teach people to remain humble when faced by their own shortcomings. Such hardships serve as reminders that perfection is for God alone. Humans are prone to make mistakes, but the prize is in seeking God's forgiveness.

5. Do Not Judge Before Hearing Both Sides

The story of the dispute that came before David, and his swift decision before hearing both sides, teaches a valuable lesson. No one should pass judgment in any matter, no matter how trivial, without first hearing both sides. Listening to only one side can lead to oppression and injustice, which may even result in severe punishment for such an oversight in this life and the next. Many fall into this habit unintentionally, so be careful not to pass one-sided judgments, rulings, or decisions.

---

[33] [Ibrahim:7]

6. The Best Earnings Are from One's Own Hands

The story of David is a reminder to try to depend on oneself. Earn an honest living, and do not covet handouts for one's livelihood. This work ethic brings people blessings and allows the world to prosper. The Prophet (s) advised us to follow David's example, as he said, "Nobody has ever eaten a better meal than that which one has earned by working with one's hands. The Prophet of God, David, used to eat from the earnings of his manual labor."[34] Remember that man was created to develop the earth, not to put himself before others.

God says

"He is the One who has revealed to you the Book (the Quran). Out of it there are verses that are Muhkamat (basic, of established meaning), which are the principal verses of the Book, and some others are Mutashabihat (whose definite meanings are unknown). Now those who have perversity in their hearts go after such part of it as is mutashabih (not of well-established meaning), seeking (to create) discord, and searching for its interpretation (that meets their desires), while no one knows its interpretation except God; and those well-grounded in knowledge say: 'We believe in it; all is from our Lord.' Only the men of understanding observe the advice."

[Al-Imran:7]

— 7 —

Moses and Al-Khidr

Wisdom and Knowledge [35]

Moses (as) was preaching to his people one day, reminding them of the signs of God. He was asked, "Who is the most knowledgeable man on earth?"

"I am," replied Moses. He assumed that as a prophet, surely he must be the most knowledgeable person in the world. But God revealed to Moses that there lived a man, at the crossing of the two seas in Yemen, who was more knowledgeable than he was.

Moses was overcome with a desire to meet and learn from this erudite man. He asked God how he could find him. God told Moses to take a cooked fish with him on his journey. Wherever he lost the fish would be the spot where the man could be found.

---

[35] Al-Qissah Al-Quraniyyah Hadayah wa Bayan, 1992, by Dr. Wahbah Al-Zuhayli.

So Moses set out on his journey in the company of a young servant. After a while, they came upon a large rock on the shore where they camped for the night. While Moses was sleeping, the servant witnessed an unbelievable sight -- the cooked fish that they had brought along flung itself into the sea. When Moses awoke, the servant forgot to mention the strange spectacle, and the pair continued on their journey.

Soon, the two travelers were overcome with hunger and weariness. Moses asked the young man to prepare a meal from part of the cooked fish. The servant remembered the miracle he had witnessed, and he explained to Moses that the fish had leaped into the sea while they were sleeping earlier.

"That is the sign I was looking for!" exclaimed Moses. The travelers retraced their steps. Soon they approached the rock by which they had camped earlier. Beside it sat a man wrapped in a cloak. His name was Al-Khidr. Moses approached him with the greeting of peace, and the man responded.

Prophet Moses informed Al-Khidr that he was the prophet of the Children of Israel.

"I have come to you so that you may teach me what knowledge you have been given," said Moses.

"You will not be able to have patience with me," replied Al-Khidr. "I have knowledge that God gave only to me, of which you are ignorant. And you have knowledge that God gave only to you, of which I am ignorant."

But Prophet Moses insisted. He was prepared to do anything to learn and abide by whatever measure of patience and obedience was required. Al-Khidr finally relented, under the condition that Moses would not ask a single question until it was time for him to explain.

The two began their journey walking along the shore. It was not long before they came upon a small port and boarded a ship to cross the sea. The poor family who owned the ship refused to take any passage fee, for they respected Al-Khidr's knowledge and piety. During their journey across the sea, Al-Khidr went to the bottom of the boat and cut a hole in its hull. When Moses expressed his shock and dismay, the wise man reminded Moses of his promise to remain silent and to refrain from asking questions. Moses immediately apologized, for he had forgotten.

As Prophet Moses and Al-Khidr sailed across the sea, a bird perched on the edge of the ship and took a sip of water with its tiny beak.

Al-Khidr remarked, "Whatever knowledge our Lord has granted you and me, compared to the infiniteness of His knowledge, it is like what this bird has drunk compared to the vastness of the sea."

After they left the ship, Moses and Al-Khidr came upon a boy playing with his friends. To Moses' shock, Al-Khidr killed the boy. Moses cried out, condemning what his companion had done. Al-Khidr reminded Moses of his promise, and Moses apologized yet again.

The two continued their journey until they reached a village. Hoping for a meal and a place to stay, the two travelers were met instead with hostility and closed doors. As they walked through the village, they came upon a crumbling wall. Al-Khidr immediately set to work repairing the broken wall.

Moses could not help himself, remarking, "Shouldn't we have asked for some compensation for fixing this wall?"

Al-Khidr told Moses that their journey together had come to an end; Moses had been unable to remain patiently silent. But before they parted, Al-Khidr explained to Moses the reasons for his actions.

"I created a small hole in the ship because there was a cruel king behind us who was confiscating every seaworthy ship. So I created a small defect in the ship to save the family from losing it entirely," Al-Khidr explained.

"As for the boy, he was the son of righteous, faithful parents. God knew the boy would grow up to torment them with his disobedience and disbelief. God wished to give them a son who would treat them better, one who would strengthen, instead of weaken, their faith," he continued.

"Finally, underneath the wall was a hidden treasure that was about to become exposed by the crumbling brick. I wished to repair the wall in order to keep the treasure hidden. This wall and treasure belonged to two orphans, children of a righteous man. God wished to protect the treasure until the orphans would reach an age when they could claim it for themselves," Al-Khidr explained.

"All of this I did with the knowledge given to me by God, not by my own choosing or judgment," Al-Khidr concluded. Leaving him to ponder the knowledge he had imparted, Al-Khidr parted ways with Moses.

Lessons Learned:

1. Pride Is from Satan

God wanted to teach Moses not to look proudly upon himself for his great knowledge, wisdom, and understanding. These qualities are from the bounties of God, and He gives them to whomever He chooses. Every blessing bestowed upon a person is purely a gift from God. Never attribute skill or talent to personal intelligence or sharp understanding. Instead, always say, "All praise to God, Who has given me this guidance and understanding." Do not give Satan a road in to corrupt one's knowledge and hard work, and God knows best.

2. A Thirst for Knowledge Is Praiseworthy

Moses taught an important lesson about the importance of seeking knowledge. He was ready and eager to always learn more, even as he grew older. God mentions about Moses' commitment, "Recall when Moses said to his young man, 'I shall not give up until I reach the meeting point of the two seas, or else I shall go on traveling for years.'"[36] No matter what level of knowledge or expertise a person may achieve, there is always room for improvement and something new to learn. Knowledge is the legacy of the prophets; it raises the status of the believer, and it determines the rank held by the righteous and the scholars. Never think that learning is completed or that the journey is over. Rather, always ask, "What can be learned next?"

3. Passion, Patience, and Following Orders Are the Basics of Learning

The story teaches that a student must first be passionate about learning. Additionally, a pupil

---

[36] [Al-Kahf:60]

44

must also work patiently through the challenges of growing intellectually. Lastly, a student must respect and follow the teacher's instructions. Moses' (as) love for learning and his intention to remain patient and obedient was mentioned in the Quran: "Moses said to him, 'May I have your company so that you teach me some of the rightful knowledge you have been given?' He said, 'You can never bear with me patiently. And how would you keep patient over something your comprehension cannot grasp?' He said, 'You will find me patient, if God wills, and I shall not disobey any order from you.'"[37] Therefore, neither force children to learn, nor rush them. Rather, instill in them a love of learning. Do not expect fast results, but be patient so that they may develop a lifelong love of education, as Moses did.

4. Curiosity and Hastiness Are Human Nature

Even as a noble prophet, Moses (as), was curious to find out who might possibly have more knowledge than he had. His curiosity led to his journey to find, follow, and learn from Al-Khidr. Furthermore, Moses could not resist interrupting his teacher, even after agreeing not to do so. Their agreement is mentioned in the Quran. "He said, 'Well, if you follow me, do not ask me about anything unless I myself start telling you about it.'"[38] For that reason, practice patience and avoid hastening, for haste is from Satan. Even the Prophet was advised against rushing: "And do not hasten with reciting the Quran before its revelation to you is concluded, and say, 'My Lord, improve me in knowledge.'"[39]

---

[37] [Al-Kahf:66-69]
[38] [Al-Kahf:70]
[39] [Taha:114]

45

5. Condemning Wrong Is a Duty

The story teaches us that we must dislike actions that are reprehensible. Although Al-Khidr insisted that Moses promise not to ask questions, Moses had to condemn the loathsome actions he had witnessed, the damaging of the boat and the slaying of the child: "He said, 'Did you slice it to drown its people? In fact, you have done a terrible act.'"[40] In addition, "He said, 'Did you kill an innocent soul while he did not kill anyone? You have committed a heinous act indeed.'"[41] As a general rule, it is an obligation to speak up and never remain silent when witnessing a wrong, and to reject it, at least in the heart, for that is the minimal and weakest form of faith.

6. Making Minor Sacrifices to Save the Greater Good

The story taught this important principle. The wisdom behind Al-Khidr's actions were later revealed. They are explained in the Quran, "As for the boat, it belonged to some poor people who worked at sea. So I wanted to make it defective, as there was a king across them who used to confiscate every boat by force.'"[42]

7. Good Parents Leave Lasting Legacies

God protected the wealth of the two orphans because of the piety of their parents. This is a reminder to every parent to work on one's own spirituality before working on one's children. Try to leave a positive, lasting effect for generations to come. God mentions specifically "…and their father was a pious man…"[43] Do not expect immediate results, for perhaps the result of one's piety might manifest itself in the distant future, as a protection and benefit for one's children.

---

[40] [Al-Kahf:71]
[41] [Al-Kahf:74]
[42] [Al-Kahf:79]
[43] [[Al-Kahf:82]

The Prophet (s) said

"Envy is permitted only in two cases: a person whom God has given wealth, and he spends it in the right way, and a person whom God has given wisdom (and knowledge), and he applies and teaches it."

Related by Abdullah Ibn Masud
(Agreed Upon)

— 8 —

A Young Scholar
Zaid Ibn Thabit [44]

Before the Battle of Badr, a bright and eager boy named Zaid Ibn Thabit (ra) asked the Prophet (s) if he could participate in the battle. The Prophet (s) turned Zaid away, for at the age of 13 he was too young and inexperienced. Zaid returned to his home in tears of disappointment.

When the battle ended and the army of believers returned victoriously to the city of Medina, the mother of Zaid, Al-Nuwar bint Malik, took her son to see the Prophet (s).

Al-Nuwar addressed the Prophet (s), "Prophet of God, this is our son, Zaid. He has memorized 17 chapters of the Quran, and he recites them just as they were revealed to you. He is bright and astute. He can read and write. Zaid wants to

[44] Al-Ilm Yasna' Al-Rijal, by Raghib Al-Sirgani.

become closer to you and hopes to use his abilities to serve you. You may listen to him if you wish."

The Prophet (s) spoke with Zaid, listened to his recitation, and tested his abilities. Then the Prophet (s) assigned him his first task.

"Zaid, learn how to write Hebrew, the language of the Jews, for I cannot trust them to correctly recount what I say," the Prophet instructed.

Zaid immediately applied himself to the new challenge and focused all of his attention on learning Hebrew.

Zaid reported, "I learned Hebrew in 17 days. I was able to speak it as though I had known it my whole life. Then I learned the Syriac language in a short time as well. I became the Prophet's translator."

Zaid began to rise among the ranks of the knowledgeable, learning from the Prophet (s) and specializing in knowledge of the Quran. His reading and writing abilities were exceptional and uncommon among many of the companions, which accelerated his pursuit of knowledge. He became the scribe of the Prophet (s) and transcribed much of the Revelation. Soon, he had memorized the entire book of God. It was uncommon to find a companion so excellent in reading and writing who had also memorized the entire Quran.

After the death of Prophet Muhammad (s), the Caliph Abu Bakr entrusted Zaid with the task of compiling the Quran into a single volume. Many of the companions who memorized the Quran had been martyred in the Battle of Yamamah. The Muslim leadership realized that the Quran needed to be compiled into an official book to avoid reliance upon human memory and personal copies, as these might deteriorate with time. This momentous and crucial task was entrusted to a young man in his early twenties. Zaid undertook the endeavor with utmost seriousness and dedication.

Umar ibn Al-Khattab (ra) used to say, "Whoever has a question about the Quran should ask Zaid Ibn Thabit." All of the companions had the greatest respect for young Zaid due to his deep knowledge of the Quran.

One day many years later, Zaid was riding through the city when Abdullah Ibn Abbas (ra), one of the most knowledgeable companions, approached Zaid and held the reins of his mount. This was a well-recognized gesture of respect. Abdullah Ibn Abbas was considered to have the deepest knowledge among the companions and was nicknamed "The Ocean" and "The Ink of the Muslims." Yet Abdullah Ibn Abbas considered Zaid to be his equal when it came to knowledge of the Revelation. The difference in age between the two scholars was only eight years.

Zaid was embarrassed by Ibn Abbas' gesture and said, "Leave the reins, nephew of the Prophet (s), may peace be upon him."

"This is how we were ordered to treat our scholars," responded Ibn Abbas.

"Give me your hand," said Zaid. He seized the hand of Ibn Abbas and kissed it, saying, "And this is how we were ordered to treat the relatives of our Prophet Muhammad, peace be upon him."

Zaid Ibn Thabit and Ibn Abbas passed away within a short time of each other.

Abu Hurairah (ra) said about the two great scholars, "Abdullah Ibn Abbas was the great successor to the great predecessor," referring to Zaid Ibn Thabit.

Lessons Learned:

1. Serve Islam in Various Ways

As a boy, Zaid thought that the only way to serve Islam was through battle, so he became upset and cried. His wise mother taught him that serving Islam could be done in a variety of ways, even by excelling in other aspects of life. Zaid perfected his work to achieve high standards and goals. The Prophet (s) said, "Indeed God loves one who, when he does a work, he does it with excellence (*itqaan*)."[45] Do not forget the shared obligation of taking on responsibilities in the community. Serving Islam is not based on the type of work one does, but rather on perfecting every endeavor and challenge with excellence, and God know best.

2. Channel Energy Appropriately

The Prophet (s) noticed that Zaid was clever, so he established priorities and utilized Zaid's intellectual gifts to complete challenging tasks. Learning the languages of neighboring societies in order to deal with them appropriately was a major necessity during this time for the emerging Muslim community. God mentions this important issue: "Oh mankind, We have created you from a male and a female, and made you into races and tribes, so that you may know one another. Surely the noblest of you, in God's sight, is the one who is most pious of you."[46] Zaid learned other languages in order to further the cause of Islam. Then he furthered his accomplishments by mastering the Quran. Make good use of time and energy, and set priorities in order to succeed.

---

[45] Tabarani.
[46] [Al-Hujaraat:13]

3. Setting Clear Goals Hastens Success

Zaid quickly and easily achieved his objectives. He set precise goals and concentrated on his noble intention to serve Islam. Zaid also allowed his sincere love for the Prophet (s) to guide him, and he found great blessings in his efforts. When aiming for success, specify goals and renew intentions. Blessings are sure to follow, God willing.

4. Writing Aids Memorization

There is no doubt that God will preserve His book, as He says, "We, Ourselves, have sent down the Remembrance (the Quran), and We are there to protect it."[47] The first Caliph, Abu Bakr (ra), made it a major priority to compile the Quran in a book after the death of the Prophet (s). He chose Zaid, who was a scholar in his own right, to lead this effort. Abu Bakr imparted an important lesson in doing so, that writing down any kind of knowledge will help others to understand, memorize, and review it. Imam Al-Shafi wrote in a poem:

Seeking knowledge is the hunt and writing is the capture,
So tie down the prey with sturdy ropes.
For it is foolish to hunt a deer,
then leave it to wander among the other creatures unleashed.

5. Respecting Scholars Make Nations Successful

The Muslim empire became the leading example for other nations. They always had tremendous respect for their scholars. This was apparent in the treatment of Abdullah Ibn Abbas, who was a scholar of the time, and who was also related to the Prophet (s). The qualities of humility, love, and respect were prevalent in the community. Noble character raises a nation up,

---

[47] [Al-Hijr:9]

but the lack of honorable qualities brings down entire nations, and God knows best.

6. Faith and Knowledge Overpower Arrogance

Abdullah and Zaid were entitled to feel proud and superior to others. However, they did not carry themselves in this manner. Faith and knowledge kept them in balance. Love, kind treatment, humility, and gratitude were the foundations of their lives. Remember, no matter how wealthy, educated, popular, or reputable a person may be, every human was created from dirt and will return one day to the dirt. Remain humble. Nothing will save a person from the final reckoning except for belief in God and good deeds, so focus on perfecting them.

7. Love and Respect for the Prophet's (s) Family

The story teaches how the companions of the Prophet (s) admired and respected his beloved family. They were generous, kind, and respectful of his relatives. God says regarding the Prophet's (s) household, "God only intends to keep (all sorts of) filth away from you, Oh members of the family (of the Prophet), and to make you pure through a perfect purification."[48] All believers must love and honor the Prophet's (s) descendents, especially those who followed in his beloved footsteps. Believers should also love the Prophet's (s) companions, following the example of righteous predecessors in this regard.

---

[48] [Al-Ahzab:33]

God says

"(Recall the time) when your Lord declared, 'If you express gratitude, I shall certainly give you more, and if you are ungrateful, then My punishment is severe.'"

[Ibrahim:7]

— 9 —

Uthman Ibn Talha and Um Salamah

God Is The Appreciative [49]

Abu Salamah and Um Salamah were some of the first Muslims to accept Islam and to attempt the migration to Medina. The husband and wife were each from noble families of the Meccan tribe of Banu Makhzum. The couple decided to leave behind the comfort, familiarity, and nobility of their positions in Mecca to join the emerging Muslim community in Medina.

As the young family set out on their brave journey, a group of Um Salamah's relatives accosted them.

They growled at Abu Salamah, "You can do what you wish with yourself, but why would we let you take our sister to strange lands far away from her tribe?"

---

[49] Al-Seerah Al-Nabawiyyah, vol. 1 pg. 468, by Ibn Hisham.

The men grabbed Um Salamah and her son, leaving Abu Salamah helpless and alone. Seeing that it was futile to rescue his wife and son from members of her own family, he trusted in God and renewed his intention to perform the migration to Medina at any cost.

Soon after, several of Abu Salamah's closest relatives also became angry with the situation.

They said, "How dare you take Um Salamah away from her husband? What makes you think you may take his son too?"

The family's relatives fought over the boy, even though they were from the same tribe. Um Salamah could only protest and watch while her husband's relatives pulled her son Salamah out of her arms. As they passionately and aggressively tugged the boy back and forth, his shoulder became dislocated.

Distraught, Um Salamah felt completely alone in Mecca. Her husband had left for Medina, her son had been ripped away from her, and the Muslims were slowly migrating away from the toxic atmosphere in Mecca. So great was her heartbreak that every day she would return to the spot where she had been torn away from her husband and child. She would spend hours there, weeping and praying, retiring only after the sun had set. Um Salamah's mournful ritual continued every day for a year.

One of Um Salamah's cousins witnessed her sorrow and took pity on her. He approached her family and asked them to allow her to reunite with her husband.

"Why don't you let this poor woman go?" he asked. "You have robbed her of both husband and child."

When they finally relented, Um Salamah's cousin interceded with her husband's family. Eventually, they allowed the child to rejoin his mother and father.

At last, Um Salamah could embrace her son again, and she was free to continue her journey to Medina. She embarked immediately, wasting not a minute in preparation, nor pausing to locate a guide. Knowing her sincerity and sacrifice, God sent an agent to escort her to where she needed to go. No one can anticipate the many means, ways, or agents of God, except for God Himself. The agent chosen for Um Salamah was a man who at that time still disbelieved in God.

The guide's name was Uthman Ibn Talha. He spotted Um Salamah alone in a place called *Tan'eem*, about five kilometers outside of Mecca. Surprised to see a noble woman of Mecca and her child unaccompanied in the desert, he approached her and inquired about her situation. Um Salamah responded that she was traveling to reunite with her husband in Medina.

"Isn't there anyone with you?" asked Uthman in disbelief.

Um Salamah declared confidently, "No, by God. There is only God, and my young son."

"Then, by God, I will not abandon you until I make sure that you reach Medina safely!" resolved Uthman.

Uthman took the reins of Um Salamah's camel and led her and her son onward. It was no small favor for a man to suddenly head out on a journey of several weeks to and from Medina. Uthman had no plan, no preparation, and no purpose, except to protect a vulnerable woman and child. He walked the 500 kilometers to Medina on foot, leading Um Salamah's camel.

When Uthman and Um Salamah finally reached Quba, a town at the outskirts of Medina, Uthman said to Um Salamah, "Your husband will be in this city. Enter it with the blessing of God." The man turned back toward the desert from whence he had come and headed alone toward Mecca, expecting neither payment nor gratitude from anyone for his service.

Um Salamah used to say, "I have not met anyone who has seen more trials than Abu Salamah, and I have not met anyone who has been more generous than Uthman Ibn Talha."

Perhaps God showed His appreciation to Uthman Ibn Talha for his service by rewarding him with the gift of Islam, seven years later.

Lessons Learned:

1. The Importance and Reward of Migration

Abu Salamah and his wife were from honorable, wealthy families, but this did not prevent them from migrating to find a suitable place to practice their faith without coercion or degradation. They were aware of the great reward as well, as God says: "So, those who emigrated, and were expelled from their homes, and were tortured in My way, and fought, and were killed, I shall certainly write off their evil deeds, and shall certainly admit them into gardens beneath which rivers flow, as a reward from God. It is God with Whom lies the beauty of the reward."[50]

2. The Negative Outcome of Family Interference

Many marital problems are magnified and escalated when well-intending family members become involved. Often parents interfere when they have no right to do so, once their children have left their homes and taken on responsibilities in their own marriages. This was the case for Um Salamah, as the family deprived her of her husband out of concern for her and her son. Yet in the process, the family harmed her and caused a painful separation that left her in agony and loneliness for a whole year. Do not interfere in marital matters that are not of one's direct concern, for this often leads to more harm than good.

3. Divisive Opinions and Resentful Relatives

Although both families came from the same tribe, this did not prevent them from allowing their pride to divide them. Instead of showing compassion to their fellow relatives and daughter-in-law, or helping her

---

[50] [Al-Imraan:195]

in the difficult separation she faced, they were driven by pride and retaliation. The family members even wrenched Um Salamah's child from her with such force that he was hurt in the process. They forgot that they were wronging the boy and his mother, and that they would be held accountable for their actions. God says, "Never think that God is unaware of what the wrongdoers are doing. He is but giving them respite up to a day when the eyes shall remain upraised (in terror)."[51] Do not be oppressive, retaliatory, or arrogant, and always stand for the oppressed, no matter what side they might be on.

4. Virtue Is Greater than Resentment

Uthman Ibn Talha was a disbeliever who did not approve of the religion of Um Salamah and Abu Salamah. Regardless, his humanity and virtuous nature compelled him to help Um Salamah, despite their religious differences. He took personal responsibility to escort her by foot from Mecca to Medina to reunite her with her husband. No matter how disliked an enemy may be, it is still no reason to abandon one's high moral ground. As God says, "Is there any reward for goodness other than goodness?"[52] The reward comes in this life before the next, God willing.

5. God Is The Appreciative, *Al-Shakur*

The loyal Uthman Ibn Talha, who did everything in his power to reunite Abu Salamah's family, never asked for any compensation or thanks. He did not even pause in Medina to see if a reward might be awaiting him there. Instead, God rewarded him by enlightening his heart with the radiance of Islam, and He would later honor him by entrusting him with the keys to the Kaaba. It was as if God taught through this man: "So that He

---

[51] [Ibrahim:42]
[52] [Al-Rahman:60]

pays them their rewards in full, and gives them more out of His grace. Surely He is Most-Forgiving, Very-Appreciative."[53]

---

[53] [Faatir:30]

God says

"Say, 'Do you worship, besides God, what has no power to do you harm or bring you benefit?' God is the All-Hearing, the All-Knowing."

[Al-Maidah:76]

— 10 —

A Woman Cries

God Hears Everything [54]

Shaikh Ali Al-Tantawi narrates this story. He says:

"I was once a judge in Syria. One evening, I was at a gathering with some friends. Inexplicably, the gathering felt suffocating and I had an overwhelming urge to go outside to get some fresh air. I asked my friends if we could leave, but they insisted on staying longer. Finally, the discomfort was so great that I excused myself to take a breath of air.

"I walked alone into the cool night. As I made my way through the dark street, I heard heartbreaking sobs. I searched to find out who was crying, moving up and down the neighborhood, until I found a woman who was weeping desperately and calling upon God for help.

---

[54] Al-Bab La Yughlaq fee Wajh As-Sa'il by Shaikh Ali Al-Tantawi.

"'Why are you crying, my sister?' I asked.

"She said, 'My husband is a harsh, unkind man. He locked me out of my home, took my children, and swore that I could never see them again. I have no place to go.'

"'Why don't you take your complaints to a judge?' I inquired.

"Her sobbing increased as she said, 'Why should a judge listen to a poor woman like me?'"

As the shaikh recounted the story, he began to cry.

He reflected, "The woman wondered how she could ever find her way to a judge, without knowing that God had dragged the judge by his collar and brought him right before her."

What kind of supplication did this poor woman make that God would answer her so quickly and directly? Those who feel any kind of despair or injustice should raise their hands to the sky and humble themselves, for He hears the call of the oppressed and will be at their side always.

Lessons Learned:

1. Keeping the Company of the Righteous Is a Form of Worship

The story begins with a reminder to spend one's time in good company. Honorable companions can strengthen faith and encourage one another to do good deeds. Umar (ra) said, "If it was not for the remembrance of God and the gathering of righteous company, I would not prefer to stay in this world of yours." Remember to make the habit of visiting your brothers and sisters in faith. Do not forget to remember God in every gathering, share pieces of advice, and tell beneficial stories so that everyone may be rewarded for keeping good company.

2. A Wife Is a Trust, so Take Good Care of Her

There is profound meaning behind a marriage contract, for each spouse is being entrusted with the responsibility of taking care of the other. As the Prophet (s) said, "Every one of you is a shepherd and is responsible for his flock. The leader of people is a guardian and is responsible for his subjects. A man is the guardian of his family and he is responsible for them. A woman is the guardian of her husband's home and his children and she is responsible for them. The servant of a man is a guardian of the property of his master and he is responsible for it. Surely, every one of you is a shepherd and is responsible for his flock."[55] A husband has no right to evict his wife. Even in a trying scenario where there are clear, irreconcilable problems, there is still a respectful way to separate so that no one may be left in a vulnerable or dangerous situation. In such circumstances, Islam elevates a

---

[55] Bukhari.

65

woman and preserves her rights. She is a trust that must be respected and well cared for by her father, husband, uncles, brothers, and sons, and God knows best.

3. Oppression Has Severe Consequences

The husband's actions were cruel and oppressive, as he expelled his wife from their home and left her vulnerable to the dangers of the night. He pushed her out of the protection of her dwelling and the safeguard of a guardian, and he further deprived her of her children. The husband forgot that God would take him to account: "Never think that God is unaware of what the wrongdoers are doing. He is but giving them respite up to a day when the eyes shall remain upraised (in terror)."[56] Never harm another person or behave oppressively, for no one escapes punishment for their oppression in the Hereafter.

4. God Is All-Hearing

God heard the cries of the oppressed woman, and He compelled the judge to leave his warm company to unknowingly wander in the night in search of her, listen to her complaint, and resolve her problem. God says, "Do they think that We do not hear their secrets and their whispers? Yes of course, Our messengers (angels) are with them who record (whatever they plan)."[57] Remember that God is always present, so never hesitate to turn to Him.

5. The Power of Supplication

Very few put into full practice the powerful tool of supplication, for it can resolve conflicts, rectify households, and make miracles happen. Draw close to God through supplication, and know that God is

---

[56] [Ibrahim:42]
[57] [Al-Zukhruf:80]

always near. He can provide a way out of any hardship. God says, "When My servants ask you about Me, then (tell them that) I am near. I respond to the call of one when he prays to Me; so they should respond to Me, and have faith in Me, so that they may be on the right path."[58]

God says

"So, (Oh Prophet) it is through mercy from God that you are gentle to them. Had you been rough and hard-hearted, they would have dispersed from around you. So, pardon them, and seek forgiveness for them. Consult them in the matter and, once you have taken a decision, place your trust in God. Surely, God loves those who place their trust in Him."

[Al-Imran:159]

— 11 —
Amarah and the Caliph
Noble Character [59]

Amarah Ibn Hamza was known throughout the land for his great character and intelligence. He was generous, trustworthy, and eloquent. Mansur, the Muslim Caliph, was aware of Amarah's reputation, and he wished to put this fine character to a test. Mansur devised a plan and appointed one of his courtiers to help him implement the scheme on the following day.

Amarah was present in the Caliph's court the next day, when a man came forward and announced, "I request an audience with the Caliph! I have been treated unjustly!" This stranger was secretly the Caliph's accomplice, who had been assigned the task of testing Amarah.

---

[59] Dalil As-Sa'ileen, pg. 197-198, by Anas Ismail Abu Dawud.

The Caliph asked, "Who has committed a crime against you?"

The man replied, "It was Amarah Ibn Hamza who wronged me."

The Caliph shot a glance at Amarah and feigned his surprise.

"How has Amarah treated you unjustly?" the Caliph questioned, pretending ignorance.

The accomplice presented his story, alleging that Amarah had unjustly stolen the claim to an exceptionally beautiful garden, which actually belonged to him. No part of the man's story was true, but the Caliph could detect no reaction upon the face of Amarah.

The Caliph commanded Amarah to leave his gathering so that he might discuss the allegation with his accuser. The Caliph would then judge between the two parties. Amarah smiled gently, without looking at the man who had made the false accusation.

"I would prefer not to leave a gathering in which the Caliph has honored me by his presence," Amarah finally remarked.

The Caliph wondered at this gracious reply, but he pretended to be angry.

"Why does this man accuse you of taking his garden?" the Caliph boomed.

<hr />

[43] [Maryam:42]

"There is no issue between us," replied Amarah politely. "If the garden really belongs to him, I will never dispute his claim to it. And if it belongs to me, I will grant it to him, as a gift, in honor of the Caliph."

At this the Caliph smiled broadly and reached for Amarah's hand.

"You have not disappointed me, Amarah!" he cried. "You are truly most noble, as people say! This was all a plan to test your character. I know that you have done no wrong. I know, indeed, that the garden is yours."

Amarah, however, insisted on giving the garden to his accuser, the caliph's accomplice.

The eyes of Amarah's accuser filled with tears as he quoted an old saying, "A container pours forth only what it holds."

Even when faced with a wrongful accusation, so noble was Amarah's heart that he could only respond with generosity and poise.

Lessons Learned:

1. ## Selecting Good Leadership Establishes Fair Nations

    The Caliph Mansur grew close to Amarah when he learned of his intelligence, righteousness, and good character. He knew that without a strong staff to implement his orders, and to fear God in their duty to the nation's citizens, their society would crumble and dissolve into conflicts and disagreements. When leading any project, select assistants who believe in the vision and who fear God. In this way success is within reach, God willing.

2. ## Testing the Leader's Council

    The wise Caliph had to test those close to him. He was able to confirm that Amarah could be trusted to properly administer important matters. The Quran teaches, "Do people think that they will be left (at ease) only on their saying, 'We believe' and will not be put to any test? Indeed We have tested those who were before them. So God will surely know the ones who are truthful, and He will surely know the liars."[60] Even in our daily affairs, it is important to periodically test assistants before assigning them weighty responsibilities. This will prevent unpleasant surprises and uncomfortable rifts, and God knows best.

3. ## Accountability Is Necessary for Justice

    Mansur wanted to hold Amarah accountable, even though the accusation was minor, and initiated by only one person. Amarah was spending time away from important responsibilities in order to defend himself and receive judgment before the Caliph. No matter

---

[60] [Al-Ankabut:2-3]

how high one might rise in rank or professional status, there are times when one may be required to defend oneself against complaints. Accept accountability for personal shortcomings, and be mindful to never oppress others by virtue of an elevated position. After all, there is responsibility in this life, but the accountability of the next life is far greater.

4. Good Character Is the Heaviest Thing in a Believer's Scale

Amarah's fine character led him to relinquish his attractive, valuable, and beloved garden, handing it over to his accuser, all to remain clear of the slightest possibility of oppression. He understood that good character is the greatest quality a believer can possess in this life and the next. As the Prophet (s) said, "Nothing is heavier upon the scale of the believer on the Day of Resurrection than good character. God truly hates a shameless, foul-mouthed person."[61] Be among those who stand proudly, holding their heads high because of their good character and kind manners, even if this means forfeiting some pleasures of this world, and God knows best.

5. A Vessel Pours Only What It Contains

Good character and noble conduct are not revealed during times of ease and comfort, but rather they show true during trying times, tests, and tribulations. Anas Ibn Malik said, "Indeed the servant will reach the highest level in Paradise due to his good character, while he was a worshipper. Another person will descend to the lowest level in Hellfire due to his bad character, while he was a worshipper." Display goodness in every situation to win Paradise, God willing.

---

[61] Tirmidhi.

6. Generosity Is Followed by Goodness

Amarah's generosity drew him closer to God, so God granted him success. He passed Mansur's test, won the praise of his accuser, and witnessed the accomplice's grateful tears of joy. God mentions, "As for the one who gives in charity and fears God, and believes in the best faith, We will facilitate for him the way to extreme ease."[62] Be honorable and generous, and be confident in a bounteous reward from God, God willing.

---

[62] [Al-Layl:5-7]

The Prophet (s) said

"I guarantee a house on the outskirts of Paradise for one who abandons arguments even if he is right, and a house in the middle of Paradise for one who abandons lies even when joking, and a house in the highest part of Paradise for one who makes his character excellent."

Related by Abu Umamah Al-Bahili
(Narrated by Abu Dawud)

— 12 —
Jabir's Camel
Kindness Shapes Communities [63]

Jabir Ibn Abdullah accompanied Prophet Muhammad (s) on *Dhat Al-Riqaa*, a military expedition. He narrated this story:

My camel was old and weak. As the expedition marched forward, my camel lagged behind, until I found myself far behind the rest of the group. The Prophet (s) noticed, and he came to join me at the back of the army.

"What's wrong, Jabir?"

I responded mournfully, "My camel is very slow."

---

[63] Hadith, Narrated by Muslim and Bukhari, Sahih.

The Prophet told me to stop the camel. He asked me to find him a stick, and so I did. The Prophet approached my camel and prodded it a few times. Then he commanded me to mount my camel and ride.

By the One who sent the Prophet (s) with the truth, my camel took off so fast that soon it was racing beside the Prophet's (s) camel! The Prophet (s) continued to converse with me as we rode.

"Would you sell your camel to me, Jabir?" asked the Prophet (s).

"Take it as a gift," I said.

The Prophet insisted, "No, sell it to me."

"How much would you offer me for it?" I asked.

"I will take it for a dirham," the Prophet (s) joked.

"That would not be a fair price, Oh Messenger of God!"

"Then for two dirhams!" the Prophet continued.

I refused the low price. The Prophet (s) continued to raise his offer until it finally reached a large sum of gold.

"Would you really agree to this price, Oh Messenger?" I asked.

"Yes," he responded.

"Then the camel is yours," I concluded.

The Prophet then asked me, "Have you gotten married yet, Jabir?"

"Yes," I answered.

"Has your wife never been married before, or is she older?"

"She is older," I said.

"Why didn't you marry a younger woman, who could joke and be playful with you, and you with her?"

I explained, "Oh Messenger of God, my father died in the Battle of Uhud. He left behind seven young daughters. I married an older woman who would help me raise and care for my younger sisters."

"You have chosen well, by the will of God," said the Prophet (s).

When I reached home, I told my wife of the conversation that had taken place with the Prophet (s), and of our agreement in regard to the camel.

She said, "We hear and we obey. Sell your camel to the Prophet (s)."

The next morning, I walked my camel to the house of the Prophet (s), as agreed, and I waited in the mosque beyond his door. When the Prophet (s) came out of his home, he found the camel waiting.

"What is this?" he asked the people.

They explained that it was the camel that Jabir had brought.

"Then where is Jabir?" asked the Prophet (s).

I approached the Prophet (s).

He said, "Come, my cousin. Take this camel -- it is now a gift from me to you."

The Prophet told Bilal to accompany me, and I was given an amount of gold, the selling price of the camel. So on that day I not only kept my camel, but I received its worth in gold as well.

Lessons Learned:

1. Treat Youth with Kindness

The Prophet (s) taught us how to treat the young, whom he honored for their foundational role in Muslim society. For this reason, he used to build bonds with young people by joking with them, talking to them, and teaching them. As was reported by Ibn Abbas, who was at most thirteen years of age at the time, "One day I was riding behind the Prophet (s) when he said, 'Young man, I will teach you some words. Be mindful of God, and He will take care of you. Be mindful of Him, and you shall find Him at your side. If you ask, ask of God. If you need help, seek it from God. Know that if the whole world were to gather together in order to help you, they would not be able to help you except if God had written so. And if the whole world were to gather together in order to harm you, they would not harm you except if God had written so. The pens have been lifted, and the pages are dry.'"[64] In our times, we find arrogant leaders who push the youth away, marginalizing them by dismissing them as inexperienced, unimportant, or ill-mannered. Be of those who care for our youth, draw them near, and treat them well. They are the heart of the Muslim community, without whom great nations will never be established or continued.

2. Think Positively to Solve a Problem

The Prophet (s) did not listen to Jabir's problem regarding his camel just to calm him down and appease him, but he actually tried to solve his problem. He even sought Jabir's assistance to find a solution by asking him to bring him a stick to prod his animal along. The

---

[64] Ahmed and Tirmidhi, Hasan and Sahih.

Prophet (s) was teaching the lesson of optimism in the face of a frustrating dilemma. Every problem has a solution in due time, so do not be narrow minded or unwilling to consider all of the possibilities. Remember that there is never a magical solution to any difficulty. By seeking God's help, relying on Him, supplicating, and showing patience, the appropriate solution will come at the right time, God willing.

3. Find Creative Ways to Aid the Poor

The Prophet (s) wanted to help Jabir, who was struggling financially with a large family to support, but it was unlikely that he would welcome charity. The Prophet (s) was able to convince Jabir to sell his camel for an enormous price by first presenting the transaction in a playful, joking manner. He then turned the matter around and presented Jabir with a gift. In this way, the Prophet (s) softened Jabir's heart and helped him, without hurting his pride or embarrassing him. As the Prophet (s) said, "Exchange gifts, and increase in your love for one another."[65] The Prophet (s) thereby displayed his great wisdom and the gentle beauty of his religion.

4. Marry Wisely

Jabir revealed that the choice of a wife should not depend upon superficial appearance or even age, as often occurs today. Rather, Jabir chose a wife of good character who could raise his children in the future, who would treat his mother and siblings properly, and who would be supportive during rough times. He chose a wife who could be patient with the faults of his family, not one who would be resentful, cause him a lifetime of trouble, or only concern herself with her own comfort. Who will learn from Jabir and heed such a lesson?

---

[65] Bukhari.

5. Good Character Makes Nations Prosper

The Prophet (s) understood that a nation could only be built on good character, good treatment of its youth, solving their problems, and involving them in its development and progress. Remember that good character and excellent work ethic shape the young into productive members of society, without whom no nation can ever be prosperous.

The Prophet (s) said

"Verily, the most beloved and closest
seated to me on the Day of Judgment are
those of you who are best in character."

Narrated by Tirmidhi

— 13 —
The Farmer in the Tree
Religion Is Based on Good Conduct [66]

Abdullah was an enthusiastic and passionate man. One day he hurried to join the noon prayer, keen on reaching the mosque on time and eager to prove his love for worship. His pace quickened as he focused on arriving before the prayer began.

On his way, Abdullah passed by some palm trees. The fronds rustled as a farmer in the treetops tended to his dates. Abdullah paused at the base of the trunk. He glared at the farmer above him. Had he not heard the call to prayer? Why was this farmer carrying on with his work as if there was no prayer to be performed?

"Come down right now! It's time for prayer!" Abdullah shouted sternly.

---

[66] Istamta' bi Hayatik, pg. 13-14, by Muhammad Abd Ar-Rahman Al-Areefi.

The farmer replied coldly, "Yes, yes," but made no motion to climb down from his trees.

Abdullah yelled out impatiently, "Hurry up and pray, you donkey!"

Abdullah's shouting startled the farmer, who grabbed a branch from the tree and began a hasty descent.

"You called me a donkey?! Who do you think you are?" shouted the farmer from above, brandishing his palm branch.

Abdullah, realizing his mistake, covered his face with his cloak and hurried in the direction of the mosque before the farmer could recognize him. When he came down from the tree, the farmer could not find the stranger who had scolded him so insolently. He threw down the branch and his tools and strode toward home to allow his temper to cool down. There, he offered the noon prayer.

Later, on his way to the afternoon prayer, Abdullah again passed by the grove of trees and spotted the farmer working in the treetops. This time, he called out cheerily.

"Assalamu alaikum! How are you doing up there?" Abdullah asked.

The farmer responded, "Very well, praise be to God."

Abdullah said, "May God bless and increase your harvest! May He grant you the reward of your effort and sacrifice for the sake of your children."

The farmer's face lit up upon hearing such kind words. He thanked Abdullah for his kind wishes.

"You have been working so hard that you did not

notice the call for the afternoon prayer, it seems," continued Abdullah. "Prayer is about to begin in the mosque. Would you like to come down, take a break, and catch the afternoon prayer? Then you can return to tending your trees. May God put more success and blessing in your work. "

The farmer agreed and calmly climbed down from the tree.

"Thank you for reminding me of prayer so kindly," said the farmer. "Now, I wish I could find the stranger who approached me earlier, so I can show him who the donkey really is!"

Lessons Learned:

1. Prayer on Time Is of the Most Beloved Acts to God

The farmer yearned to complete his prayers on time, proving that he understood that the call to prayer, the *athaan*, is an announcement that a servant is about to speak to his Lord. Delaying prayer decreases a servant's complete reward. For that reason, the Prophet (s) declared that prayer on time is one of the most beloved acts before God. When asked by Abdullah Ibn Masud regarding the actions most pleasing to God, the Prophet (s) replied, "The most beloved of deeds according to God is prayer in its right time, then to treat parents in an excellent manner, and then to struggle (*jihad*) in the path of God."[67] Build the habit and desire to complete each prayer at the beginning of its appointed time, for God awaits His servants.

2. Gentle, Caring Advice Is Often Accepted

Most people try to advise those close to them. They act out of sincere concern, to warn those who might stumble and make terrible mistakes. Unfortunately, all too often they fail to give advice in a gentle and tolerable way. Most people resist criticism. It is human nature to dislike the unpleasantness of feeling insulted, and no one likes to look weak, or to have embarrassing shortcomings exposed in front of others. When offering advice, utilize kind words and tactful phrases, and make the suggestions as palatable as possible. Show compassion before posing advice, and remember to offer suggestions in private. Lastly, renew intentions to keep them pure and to show sincere care.

---

[67] Agreed upon.

3. Good Character Is the Essence of Religion

Abdullah mercifully approached the farmer in their second encounter. He inquired regarding his well-being and his work, and he gently encouraged the farmer to attend prayer in the mosque. Abdullah's gracious manner clearly influenced the farmer's agreeable response. Early Muslims mastered the art of gentle persuasion, and they used tactful strategies and noble character to compel an expansive proliferation of faith worldwide. God affirms, "So, (Oh Prophet) it is through mercy from God that you are gentle to them. Had you been rough and hard-hearted, they would have dispersed from around you. So, pardon them, and seek forgiveness for them. Consult them in the matter and, once you have taken a decision, place your trust in God. Surely, God loves those who place their trust in Him."[68] Remember that religion is all about good conduct. Good character will earn God's love, as well as the love of people, God willing.

4. Likening People to Dishonorable Things Is Offensive

When Abdullah called the man a donkey, the farmer was prepared to strike him for calling him a name that was degrading, disrespectful, and implied a lack of intelligence. Such name-calling was prohibited by the Prophet (s), who said, "The believer does not taunt others, he does not curse others, he does not use profanity, and he does not abuse others."[69] Refrain from harming others with belittling words and distasteful titles, yet try to pardon those who carelessly do so.

---

[68] [Al-Imran:159]

[69] Tirmidhi.

God says

"Their sides remain apart from their beds. They call their Lord with fear and hope, and they spend (in charity) out of what We have given to them. So, no one knows the eyes' delight that has been reserved for them in secret, as a reward for what they used to do."

[Al-Sajdah:16-17]

— 14 —
Umar Ibn Al-Khattab and the Old Woman
Fear of God [70]

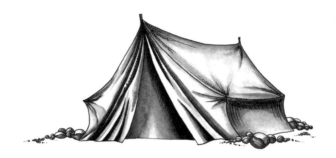

Umar Ibn Al-Khattab, the Muslim Caliph, returned to Medina from a trip to Syria. Upon his arrival, he secluded himself from company, choosing to walk alone, unrecognized in the streets of Medina. It was his habit to walk anonymously among the inhabitants in order to discover those who were suffering or in need. As he roamed the neighborhoods, he saw an old woman camping in a tent. He approached the tent quietly, but she noticed him from a distance and called out.

"Hey you, sir! What news do you have of Umar?" she beckoned.

"He has returned safely from Syria," responded Umar.

[70] Samt An-Nujoom Al-Awali by Imam Al-Asami; Al-Riyadh An-Nadirah by Muhib At-Tabari.

The woman shook her head firmly, muttering, "May God not reward him! No regards to him from me!"

"Why do you say such things?" asked Umar.

"Because, ever since he has ruled Muslim affairs, I have received neither a dinar nor a dirham of assistance," she complained sorely.

"But how could Umar know of your need?" asked the disguised Caliph.

"How could someone rule over a land and not know, from east to west, the condition of everyone within?" the woman questioned in astonishment.

At the woman's exclamation, Umar wept, "Woe to Umar! Even the old women complain about him!"

Then Umar asked the woman, "Oh servant of God, for what price could I repair the wrongs that Umar has done? How much would it cost to satisfy your needs? I only wish to save Umar from the fire."

"Are you joking with me?" she asked.

"Not in the least," responded the Caliph. He continued to plead with the woman until he had agreed to pay the elderly woman a generous sum. As he completed the negotiations, Ali Ibn Abi Talib and Abdullah Ibn Masud happened to pass by.

"*Assalamu alaikum*, Oh Leader of the Believers," they greeted Umar.

The woman slapped her forehead and exclaimed, "Oh my! I have insulted the Leader of the Believers to his face!"

"Do not worry," Umar consoled her. He searched his pockets for money, trying to gather the amount needed. He then tore a piece from his woolen cloak and wrote upon it:

"In the Name of God, the Most Merciful, the Most Compassionate. This is a contract by which Umar has satisfied your complaints against him for the sum of 25 dinars. Whatever your claim against him might be on the Day of Resurrection, he is free from those claims. Witness to this are Ali Ibn Abi Talib and Abdullah Ibn Masud."

Umar handed the woolen contract to one of his companions and said, "If I die, wrap this in my shroud, so I may meet my Lord with it."

Lessons Learned:

1. Rulers Are Responsible to Meet the Needs of the People

Umar (ra) was eager to satisfy the needs of the citizens and to learn about their complaints. Therefore, when he returned to Medina after a short period away, he went directly to the people he governed to see what problems they might have encountered during his absence. He understood that he was responsible for his people, and that he would be asked about them on the Day of Judgment. As God mentioned, "So, We shall ask those to whom the messengers were sent, and We shall ask the messengers (how they conveyed the message]."[71] As the prophets were sent to guide their people, those in positions of authority are also required to care for the citizens whom they govern. When assuming a leadership role, remember to seek feedback from those for whom you are responsible, and help fulfill their needs. Show compassion in this world to prepare for the next.

2. Personal Accountability Is a Quality of the Believer

The elderly woman's criticism brought tears of fear to Umar's eyes, as he felt he had been inadequate in meeting her needs. Umar understood that he would be taken into account before God for every large or small action perpetrated in the nation he led. God speaks of this: "And the book (of deeds) will be placed (before them), then you will see the guilty people scared of its contents and saying, 'Woe to us! What a book is this! It has missed nothing, minor or major, but has taken it into account.' Thus they will find whatever they did present before them, and your Lord will not wrong

---

[71] [Al-Araf:6]

anyone."[72] Keep intentions pure, do good work, be truthful, and examine one's own actions. Seek God's forgiveness, for God is Oft-Forgiving.

3. **Compensating Those Wronged Is the First Step in Repentance**

Umar ibn Al-Khattab (ra) taught that after inflicting harm, intentionally or unintentionally, it is necessary to seek pardon and forgiveness. Umar took it one step further, paying a monetary price to convert his verbal apology into a physical one. He compensated the oppressed woman for what she had suffered due to his negligence. Be careful to avoid oppressing others. But if one makes a mistake, ask for God's forgiveness, and make amends with those who were wronged. Be mindful to do so before the Day of Judgment, because oppression is no small matter in this life or the next.

4. **Fearing God Leads to Paradise**

Umar's (ra) deep fear of God made him ask the elderly woman to name a price for her suffering. It also made him draw up a contract of forgiveness between them, for which he included witnesses, and he gave instructions to bury the contract in his grave. The closer a servant grows to the Lord, the more accountable and scrupulous the servant will become about his or her own actions. Fear is useful, for it reminds one to yearn for Paradise. God says: "Whereas for the one who feared to stand before his Lord, and restrained himself from the (evil) desire, Paradise will be the abode."[73] Compete in every way to earn Paradise, even if that means apologizing or paying a fine. Remember that the path to God's forgiveness is set with trials, and that the final reward is in Paradise.

---

[72] [Al-Kahf:49]
[73] [Al-Naziaat:40-41]

God says

---

*"It is none but Satan who frightens (you)
of his friends. So, do not fear them; but
fear Me, if you are believers."*

[Al-Imran:175]

— 15 —

Ants on the Trees

The Cautious and God-Fearing[74]

Sultan Sulaiman Al-Qanuni was the ruler of the Ottoman Empire. It is said that two servants at the Topkapi Palace found trees in the garden which were infested with ants. The palace gardeners recommended coating the branches of the trees with lime, which would kill the insects.

It was the policy of the Sultan to always consult the top religious scholars of the land before implementing any new measures. The Sultan personally went to seek the council of Abu Al-Su'ood Afandi about coating the tree branches with lime, but he was unable to locate him. So the Sultan left a letter, in the form of lines of poetry, on the door of the scholar's home. The letter read:

---

[74] Qissa wa Fikra by Dr. Tariq Al-Suwaidan, and Min Siyar Salateen Ad-Dawla Al-Aliyyah Al-Uthmaniyah, 15-40.

When the ants pervade the tree,
Blame for killing them shall there be?

Abu Al-Su'ood soon wrote a letter in response:

When the scales of justice are forth brought,
Even the ant fearlessly takes its right as sought.

The Sultan was well aware that he had many concerns that were more critical than an infestation of ants. However, he was responsible for ruling an entire nation with justice, which did not exclude the ants on the trees. As was his custom, the Sultan continued to seek a fatwa, or religious ruling, for every issue he faced, whether big or small. Given the ruling in regard to the ants, the Sultan left them in peace.

When the Sultan died in the Battle of Zeektur, his body was brought back to Constantinople, the capital of the Ottoman Empire. In his will, the Sultan requested that he be buried with a small box. The scholars were puzzled by this request, and they assumed that the container stored money or treasure. When they opened it, they were amazed to discover hundreds of pieces of paper upon which were written all of the religious rulings the Sultan had solicited during his reign. He wished to be buried with these papers so that he would be prepared to defend himself before God. If the religious scholars of his age had approved the legal measures contained in the box, the Sultan had hoped that he would be pardoned from blame on the Day of Judgment.

Upon seeing the box of papers, the head scholar, Shaikh Abu Su'ood, wept.

"You have saved yourself, Sultan Sulaiman," the scholar mourned. "But what sky will shade us, and what earth will hold us, if we have made mistakes in our rulings?"

Such were the scholars of those times, and such were the rulers.

Lessons Learned:

1. The Council of Scholars Is Vital for Successful Nations

Sultan Sulaiman sought the council of scholars in regard to a trivial matter: ants defacing trees on the palace grounds. This example shows how nations should depend upon sacred law for their rulings and judgments. Consultation between rulers and scholars is essential for success. God describes the importance of consultation, and He mentions "… those who have responded to their Lord (in submission to Him), and have established prayer, and whose affairs are (settled) with mutual consultation between them, and who spend out of what We have given to them, and those who, when they are subjected to aggression, defend themselves."[75] Therefore, before taking any position, research and verify that it is sound according to sacred law. If a clear answer is hard to find, then seek council, for no one who seeks the truth will be disappointed.

2. The Prohibition of Burning Ants

Although exterminating the ants would have protected the trees, the council warned that doing so would cause later misfortune to the person who killed them. The Prophet (s) spoke of this: "An ant had bitten a prophet (one amongst the earlier prophets) and he ordered that the colony of the ants should be burned. Then God revealed to him, 'Because of an ant's bite, you have burned a community from amongst the communities which sings My glory.'"[76] Therefore, avoid harming, torturing, or killing any insect, animal, or human, for the oppressed will hold their oppressors accountable on the Day of Judgment.

---

[75] [Al-Shura:38-39]
[76] Bukhari and Muslim.

3. Documenting and Safeguarding Records

Sultan Sulaiman meticulously recorded every ruling and transaction that occurred during his reign. His example teaches us that soliciting and verifying information is important, and that documentation is even more important. Words change from time to time, and intentions can alter after a mutual agreement has been made. For this reason, it is essential to keep records, for they can serve as written proof in front of God, the scholars, and people. Keeping documentation might also lighten one's responsibility for a decision made in accordance with the ruling of another party. For this reason, record and safeguard important information, in order to stand before God with little fear.

4. Fear of God Leads to Scrupulousness

Sultan Sulaiman desired to preserve the rulings which he sought, and he asked that they be buried with him in his grave. His actions give evidence to his strong sense of accountability, scrupulousness, and his fear of God. At the same time, God says, "But whoever does righteous deeds, while he is a believer, shall fear neither injustice nor curtailment (of his rewards)."[77] Seek council, set noble intentions, do righteous deeds, and do not fear oppression on the Day of Judgment. In the words of the All-Merciful, "Surely, God does not wrong people at all, but the people do wrong their own selves."[78]

5. The Integrity of a Nation Relies upon Commanding Good and Forbidding Evil

The scholar Abu Al-Su'ood Afandi showed integrity as he forbade evil in a tactful and gracious manner.

---

[77] [Taha:112]
[78] [Yunus:44]

Furthermore, he wept out of fear of God, and he realized the gravity of his role in offering Islamic rulings. It is the integrity of scholars and rulers which prepares a nation for greatness. God says, "You are the best nation ever raised for mankind. You command the good and forbid the evil, and you believe in God."[79] Be among those who encourage right and discourage wrong, branches on the tree of integrity, in support of a greater nation.

---

[79] [Al-Imraan:110]

Other Titles by the Author

Volume 1 - Short Stories to Warm the Heart

The Virtues of Reading Quran * Live by the Verses of the Quran * Quran is Light * Quran for Healing * The Importance of Prayer (Martyrdom of 'Umar) * The Importance of Perfecting Prayer * The Importance of Friday Prayer * Reverence in Prayer * The Importance of Fajr Prayer * The Importance of Praying with a Group * Midnight Prayers * Honesty Is Your Protector * Being Truthful with the Prophet (PBUH) * The Price of Honesty * God is the Creator (Abu Hanifa and the Athiest)

Volume 2 - Kindness to Family, Supplication, and Other Short Stories to Warm the Heart

The Act of Sincerity * How Can I Be Good to My Mother? * Kindness to Parents * Dear to God, Dutiful to Parents * God Is the Merciful * God, the Giver of Life * Fasting and Higher Consciousness * The Reward for the Fasting * Supplication Is the Heart of Worship * Supplication: Relief from Distress * The Acceptance of True Supplication * The Etiquette of Eating * The Food of the Generous Is Medicine * Charity Begins at Home * The Fruits of Maintaining Bonds of Kinship

Volume 3 - Charity, Creation, and Other Short Stories to Warm the Heart

Piety and the Heart * Reaching God Through Virtuous Deeds * Consciousness of God * God is the Provider * God Is Ever-Witnessing * Belief in Judgment Day * Prosperous Charity * The Charity of Words * Charity and Growing Wealth * Shame Before God * The Best to Hire Is the Strong and Trustworthy * Arrogance, the Root of Trouble * The First Trial * The Importance of Giving Charity (Zakah) * The Recipients of Charity (Zakah)

Volume 4 - Compassion, Brotherhood, and Other Short Stories to Warm the Heart

A Lesson in Humility * The Anonymous Helper * The Mystery Worshipper * One Spoonful * 99 Murders * Catching the Fish * The Missing Finger * Marketplace Greetings * The Emperor's Rock * Rescuing a Sinner * The Story of Abraham * Sarah's Journey Through Egypt * The Pilgrimage * The Visit for God * The Loyal Friend

Notes

Notes

Notes

Notes

Notes